JUMBO JACK'S COOKBOOKS

AUDUBON MEDIA CORPORATION
301 BROADWAY • AUDUBON IA 50025
1-800-798-2635

Dedicated to:

Uncle Virgil, who had some of the best eatin' apples around.

APPLES!

APPLES!

APPLES!

© by M. Mosley 1997

3

Heart Huggin' 'N Tummy Warmin'
recipes from

HEARTS & TUMMIES
COOKBOOK COMPANY
-a Dinky Division of Quixote Press

(800) 571-BOOK
(319) 372-7480

SO, WHAT'S SO SPECIAL ABOUT COOKING WITH APPLES?

Well, I guess there isn't anything particularly special about the cooking you can do with apples.... that is, unless you want some of the best dang eatin' in this corner of the universe. That's all that's special. And, I didn't just collect a bunch of apple recipes and string 'em together to make this book. These recipes are the best out of my own kitchen, Mom's kitchen and from the kitchens of lots of years of neighbors who gave me the best they had.

TABLE OF CONTENTS

APPETIZERS
&
BEVERAGES

HOLIDAY CIDER

6 sticks cinnamon
16 cloves, cut up
1 tsp. whole allspice
2 orange slices

6 C. apple juice or cider
2 C. cranberry juice cocktail
4 C. sugar

Put cinnamon, cloves and allspice in bag. Simmer all ten minutes. Take out bag and oranges. Add 1 C. rum (optional). Pour over round peppermint candy in a cup and serve hot.

APPLE BRANDY COOLER

2½ oz. brandy
1 oz. light rum
4 oz. apple juice

½ oz. lime juice
1 tsp. dark rum
1 slice lime

Shake brandy, light rum, apple juice, lime juice and ice well. Strain into a tall 14-ounce glass. Add ice to fill glass. Stir, and float the dark rum on top of drink. Add lime slice for garnish. Makes 1 large drink.

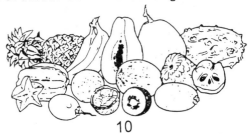

10

APPLE CHEESE SLICES

4 oz. blue vein cheese
2 T. butter
2 T. brandy

4 red apples, sliced
1 T. water
1 T. lemon juice

Blend the cheese, butter and brandy together; cover and chill several hours. Cut the unpeeled apples, removing core, dip in lemon water to prevent discoloration. Drain and dry apples, spread one side with the cheese mixture and arrange on a platter; serve cold.

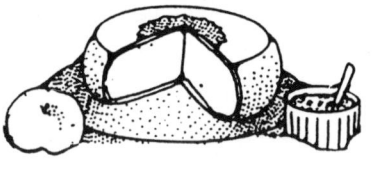

11

Beverage Fix-Ups

lemonade
apple juice
cinnamon stick or lemon juice

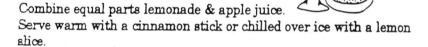

Combine equal parts lemonade & apple juice.
Serve warm with a cinnamon stick or chilled over ice with a lemon slice.

Hot Cider Punch

2 C. cranberry juice
8 C. apple cider
1/4 C. brown sugar

2 cinnamon sticks
3/4 T. whole cloves
1/4 tsp. salt

Place juice and cider in electric perculator. Place oll other ingredients in basket Perk till it shuts off. For a 30 cup pot, use 1 gallon cider, 1 quart cranberry juice, and triple the spices.

Cider Punch

1 qt. sweet cider
1 qt. club soda

Juice of 3 lemons
Sugar to taste (about ½ C.)

Add club soda after you have it all mixed in bowl with ice.

14

Hot Spiced Cider

½ gal. apple cider
2 sticks cinnamon (whole)
8 cloves (whole)

5 allspice (whole)
2 T. brown sugar
1 shake cinnamon (ground)

Put all ingredients in large pan and boil for 5 minutes, stirring once or twice.

15

APPLE DIP

8 oz. cream cheese
¼ C. white sugar
¾ C. brown sugar

¼ - ½ C. chopped pecans
1 tsp. vanilla

Blend well and serve with apple wedges.

MULLED CIDER

1 gallon apple cider
1 C. brown sugar

2 stp. whole allspice
3 cinnamon sticks

Heat apple and brown sugar to a slow boil and shut off. Then add remaining ingredients. Cover and let sit for 20 minutes. Drain and store in refrigerator. Reheat to serve.

FROTHY APPLE PUNCH

3 C. apple juice or apple cider
  (chilled)
⅓ C. orange juice (chilled)
2 C. light cream

3 egg whites
⅓ C. sugar
Ground cinnamon

In a large mixing bowl combine apple juice or cider and orange juice. Add cream and beat with a rotary beater till frothy. In a small mixer bowl, beat egg whites on high speed of electric mixer till soft peaks form (tips curl over). Gradually add sugar, beating till stiff peaks form (tips stand straight). Gently fold egg whites into cider-cream mixture, leaving a few fluffs of egg white. Pour into a punch bowl. Sprinkle cinnamon atop. To serve, ladle into punch cups. Serve immediately. Makes 8 (6 oz. each) servings.

MULLED CIDER PUNCH

2 qt. apple cider or juice
1 C. apricot nectar
1 C. orange juice

½ tsp. cinnamon
Orange slices

In saucepan, combine cider, nectar, orange juice and cinnamon; heat and stir. Garnish with orange slices.

19

MAIN DISHES

BAKED APPLES

1 C. sugar (brown or white)
1 C. water
½ C. butter

¼ C. flour
1 tsp. cinnamon
Baking apples

Butter 9x13-inch pan, fill ¾ full of apples that have been quartered. Mix rest in ingredients and pour over the apples. Bake at 350° for 45 minutes, or until tender.

BAKED APPLES WITH MARSHMALLOWS

1 T. flour
⅔ C. sugar
8 apples
Cinnamon to taste

2 C water
Red food coloring
Miniature marshmallows
Nuts

Butter pan. Add flour, sugar and small amount of cinnamon. Core 8 solid apples. Arrange over above ingredients. Add a few drops red food coloring to 2 C water. Pour over apples. Bake 350° 1½ hours. While hot garnish with miniature marshmallows and pieces of nuts.

RED HOT BAKED APPLES

4-6 apples
1 ½ C. sugar

1 C. water
½ C. cinnamon candy

Halve apples and core. Put in 8-inch square baking dish, cut side down. Boil sugar, water and red hots for 1 minute. Pour over apples and bake in 350° oven until tender. Better if it sets overnight to absorb syrup.

OVEN APPLE TOAST

4 slices bread   1 apple
cinnamon   butter

Butter 4 slices of bread and put on a baking sheet. Slice the apple very thin.
Put the apple slices on the bread. Sprinkle with cinnamon. Bake 10 to 12
minutes at 375°.

26

LEMONY BAKED APPLES

2 large apples, cored
3 oz. frozen lemonade concentrate, thawed
1 Tsp. brown sugar

Peel apples 1/3 down from the stem end. Arrange in greased shallow baking dish. Spoon concentrate into cavities and over tops of apples. Sprinkle with brown sugar. Bake at 350° (basting occasionally,) for 45 minutes or until apples are tender, but retain their shapes. Serve warm or at room temperature with baking juices.

BAKED APPLES A LA ORANGE

2 red apples
1/4 cup orange juice
1 Tsp. brown sugar

dash nutmeg
1 Tbs. chopped walnuts (optional)
1/2 tsp. grated orange peel

Preheat oven to 375° Wash and core apples. Remove strip of peel from around center. Place in 8-inch square baking dish. In small bowl, combine orange juice, brown sugar, orange peel and nutmeg. Pour over apples. Cover and bake at 375° for 25 minutes. Baste apples, sprinkle with nuts. Continue baking, uncovered, for 20 to 25 minutes or until apples are tender. Spoon sauce over apples to serve.

Microwave Directions: Prepare apples and sauce as above. Cover with plastic wrap. Microwave on High for 6 minutes, rotating dish 1/4 turn every 2 minutes. Baste with sauce. Sprinkle with nuts. Continue microwaving for 3 to 4 minutes or until apples are tender.

28

Sausage With Apples

1 lb. link sausage
6 medium onions
Salt
Pepper

Paprika
6 medium sweet potatoes
6 apples
  (pared, cored & halved)

Cover sausage with cold water and boil; drain. Place sausage in large baking dish. Cover with pared sweet potatoes and onions. Season with salt, pepper, and paprika. Cover and bake at 400° for 1 hour; uncover. Add apples and cover. Bake slowly until fruit is tender. Serve at once. Serves 6.

29

APPLE LOAF

1/2 C. soft shortening
2/3 C. brown sugar (packed)
2 eggs
1 C. thick applesauce
2 C. flour

1 tsp. baking powder
1/2 tsp. salt
1 tsp. soda
1/2 C. chopped nuts

Cream brown sugar, shorting, and eggs; stir in applesauce. Sift together flour, baking powder, soda, and salt; add to creamed mixture. Add chopped nuts and pour into greased bread pan and bake at 350° for 50 to 55 minutes.

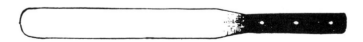

Applesauce Meatballs

2 c. crushed cornflakes
3 T. chopped onion
1½ lbs. ground beef
1½ tsp. salt
Pepper, to taste

1 egg
⅔ C. applesauce
1 can tomato soup*
½ can water*
¼ C. ketchup*

Mix cornflakes, onion, ground beef, salt, pepper, egg, and applesauce. Shape into 24 balls and place in a 13x9-inch pan. Cover with tomato soup, water, and ketchup. Bake at 350° for 1 hour. (*Can use ¼ C. ketchup and tomato juice to cover meatballs at least 2½ cups. More tomato juice can be added, if desired.)

31

SALADS & SAUCES

GRANDMA'S APPLESAUCE

4 C. pared, roughly chopped apples
1/4 C. orange juice
1 small dollop of butter or Margarine

approximately 1 C. sugar
1/2 tsp. ground cinnamon
1/4 tsp. ground nutmeg

As you pare and chop the apples into pieces, put them in a 2 quart sauce pan and sprinkle with the orange juice to keep them from turning brown. Add the sugar, taking into account the tartness of the apples, and adjusting the amount of sugar to taste. Add cinnamon and nutmeg, mixing with large spoon to coat the apple pieces well. Cook gently over a medium heat, stirring frequently to keep from sticking. When tender, remove from heat and mash with fork or potato masher to desired consistency . Taste for sweetness and add more sugar if desired. To give extra richness to the flavor, add a small dollop of butter or margarine and stir until completely melted and thoroughly incorporated into the sauce. Allow to cool for a while, then pour into lidded plastic container, or glass jar to keep in the refrigerator.

Apple Raisin Slaw

1½ C. unpeeled, cored & diced
  red apples
2 C. shredded cabbage

⅓ C. seedless raisins
½ C. coleslaw dressing

Mix thoroughly the apples, cabbage, raisins, and dressing. Serves 4.

APPLE CRUNCH SALAD

2 (3 oz. ea.) pkgs. strawberry flavored
  gelatin
2 C. boiling water
1½ C. apple juice or cider

¼ tsp. cinnamon
1 C. diced & peeled apples
½ C. diced celery
¼ C. chopped pecans

Dissolve gelatin in boiling water. Add apple juice and cinnamon. Chill until slightly thickened; fold in apples, celery, and nuts. Spoon into 6-cup mold.

36

APPLE SLAW

3 C. finely shredded cabbage
½ C. diced celery
½ C. mayonnaise
1 T. sugar
1 tsp. salt
2-3 T. vinegar

½ tsp. celery seed
2 C. diced unpeeled red apples
½ C. miniature marshmallows
Paprika
Chopped walnuts (optional)

Combine cabbage and celery. Mix together mayonnaise, sugar, salt, vinegar and celery seed; add to cabbage and celery mixture and toss together until well mixed. Add diced apples and marshmallows. Toss again, lightly. Top with a dash of paprika. Walnuts may be added for extra flavor. Serves 6-8.

CABBAGE AND APPLE SALAD

1 pkg. lemon Jell-o
4 tsp. vinegar
½ tsp. salt

1 C. shredded cabbage
1 C. diced apples
¼ C. chopped
    sweet pickle

Dissolve Jell-o in 1 pt. hot water. Add the vinegar and salt. Chill until slightly thickened then fold in the cabbage, apples, and sweet pickle. Mold and chill Serves 6.

38

Breads, Etc.

Apple Bread

½ C. oil
2 eggs
1 C. sugar
1½ C. all-purpose flour
½ tsp. baking soda
1½ C. diced peeled apples

¼ tsp. salt
½ C. chopped nuts
1 tsp. vanilla
½ tsp. cinnamon
½ tsp. nutmeg

Mix first 3 ingredients together. Add remaining ingredients and mix. Turn into greased and floured 8x4-inch loaf pan. Bake at 300° for 1½ hours. Cool for 10 minutes. Remove from pan. Cool on rack for 10 minutes. Wrap in foil while still warm.

41

Dutch Apple Bread

½ C. shortening (no butter)
1 C. granulated sugar
2 eggs
1 C. coarsely chopped apples
   (peeled)

2 C. all-purpose flour (sifted)
1½ T. sour milk
1 tsp. baking soda
½ tsp. salt
1 tsp. vanilla

Cream shortening and sugar; add the eggs and beat. Add the chopped apples. Add the flour and beat well. Mix the sour milk with the soda. Add to batter. Add the salt and vanilla; beat. Put in two 4x8-inch greased pans. Top with mixture of 2 tablespoons and ½ tsp. cinnamon. Bake at 350° for 50 to 60 minutes. NOTE: Nutmeats may also be added.

APPLE BREAD

Beat:
3 eggs
2 C. sugar
1 C: oil
Then add:
3 C. flour

1 tsp. salt
1 tsp. cinnamon
2 tsp. vanilla
1 tsp. soda
3 C. raw apples (chopped fine)
1 C. pecans (chopped)

Bake 1 hour, 5 minutes at 325° in 2 loaf pans. Sprinkle sugar over top before baking. Very moist.

FRUIT MIX

1½ C. brown sugar
½ C. butter
2 eggs (beaten)
¼ C. milk
2 C. flour (sifted)
1 tsp. soda
¼ tsp. salt
¼ tsp. ginger
½ tsp. nutmeg

¾ tsp. cinnamon
1 C. currants
⅔ C. seedless raisins (chopped)
⅔ C. chopped dates
½ C. diced candied pineapple
12 candied cherries (chopped)
2 T. chopped citron
1 C. chopped raw apples
½ C. chopped nutmeats

(more)

44

(continued)

Cream together brown sugar, butter and eggs; add milk. Sift 1/2 C. of the flour over the fruit and nut mixture. Sift remaining flour, spices, salt, and soda together; add to the creamed mixture along with the fruit mixture. Mix until you can see no more flour. This can be a cookie or cake. Drop cookies on a sheet and bake at 350° for 1 hour and 20 minutes. I have bought the pre-pakaged candied fruit mix and added the other fresh fruit. It makes a beautiful looking and tasting cake or bread in a loaf pan. Nice at Christmas.

PECAN APPLE BREAD

1/2 C. margarine (softened)
1 C. sugar
2 eggs
2 Tbs. milk
1 tsp. vanilla
1/4 tsp. butter or butter flavoring

1/4 tsp. lemon extract
2 C. flour
1 tsp. baking power
1 tsp. soda
1 C. chopped apples
1/2 C. pecans

Cream 1/2 C. margarine and sugar together. Add rest of ingredients and mix well. Turn into greased loaf pan and bake at 350° for about 1 hour. Yields 1 loaf.

APPLESAUCE NUT BREAD

2 C. flour minus 2 T.
¾ C. sugar
2 tsp. baking powder
½ tsp. soda
½ tsp. salt

1 tsp. cinnamon
1 egg
¼ C. margarine
1½ C. applesauce
1 C. nuts

Mix ingredients just enough to moisten. Bake 1 hour at 325°.

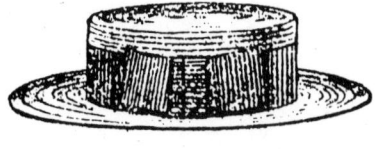

Applesauce Bread Pudding

8 slices day old white bread
2 C. applesauce
½ tsp. cinnamon
½ C. brown sugar
2 eggs

2½ C. milk
½ tsp. vanilla
¼ tsp. salt
Margarine

Spread one side of each slice of bread with margarine. If desired, remove crusts. Arrange 4 slices of bread, buttered side up, in a greased 8x8-inch square pan or baking dish. Mix together applesauce, cinnamon, and 2 T. of brown sugar. Spread over bread in dish. Cut each remaining slice of bread into four triangles and arrange on filling in baking dish covering entire surface. Beat together eggs, milk, vanilla, salt, and remaining brown sugar. Pour over bread and sprinkle with additional cinnamon. Bake at 350° or 325° for glass for 50 to 55 minutes. Can be served with milk, ice cream or whipped topping.

German Apple Pancakes

½ C. + 1 T. flour
½ tsp. baking powder
¼ tsp. salt
6 large eggs (separated)
1 C. sugar (divided - ¾ C and ¼ C.)
½ C. + 1 T. milk
1 tsp. vanilla

¼ C. lemon juice
3 C. pared and finely diced apples
4 T. butter
1 tsp. cinnamon
(mix with ¼ C. sugar)
Lemon juice and sugar for extra
   topping, if desired

(more)

49

(continued)

In large bowl, sift together flour, baking powder and salt; set aside. In another large bowl, beat egg whites until foamy. Gradually add ¾ C. sugar and continue beating until mixture forms stiff peaks; set aside. In small bowl, beat egg yolks until thickened. Beat in milk and vanilla. Combine milk mixture with reserved flour mixture, beating until smooth. Sprinkle lemon juice on apples and stir so apples are well coated. Fold reserved egg white mixture with apple mixture into flour-milk batter until well combined. In large 12-inch or 14-inch skillet, melt butter. Pour in pancake mixture and sprinkle with remaining quarter cup sugar and cinnamon. Bake at 375° for 15-20 minutes or until pancake is set and tests done, like a custard. Cut into large wedges and serve with extra lemon juice and sugar, if desired. Makes 6 servings.

GERMAN APPLE-EGG PANCAKES

4 eggs (separated)	Dash of salt
1 C. milk	1 large apple (peeled and
1¼ C. sifted flour	· thinly sliced)
2 T. sugar	1 can applesauce

Separate eggs; beat egg whites until foamy. To the egg yolks add milk, flour, sugar, salt. Mix well. Fold in egg whites and apple slices last. Fry pancakes in well greased frying pan. Top panccakes with hot applesauce to serve. Will serve 3-4 persons.

APPLE NUT BREAD

1 C. sugar	½ tsp. salt
½ C. Wesson Oil	1 tsp. soda
2 eggs	3 T. orange juice
1 C. chopped apples	½ tsp. vanilla
2 C. flour	½ C. chopped nuts

Cream sugar and shortening. Beat eggs in well, then add apples, dry ingredients, juice, vanilla, and nutmeats. Bake in loaf pan for around 80 to 90 minutes (test with a toothpick) at 300°. Note: Line loaf pan with waxed paper. Freezes nicely. Really good at holiday time or anytime.

Applesauce-Carrot Muffins

½ C. raisins
1 C. all-purpose flour
¾ C. whole-wheat flour
1 tsp. baking soda
½ tsp. salt
1 tsp. cinnamon
½ tsp. nutmeg (optional)

1 large egg
½ C. sugar
¼ C. oil
1 tsp. vanilla
¼ tsp. lemon extract
1 C. applesauce
¾ C. grated carrots

Combine raisins with ½ C. warm water in small bowl; let soak. Mix flours, soda, salt, and spices in large bowl. Beat egg and sugar in second bowl until fluffy; beat in oil, vanilla, and lemon. Stir in applesauce. Stir applesauce mixture into flour until just blended. Quickly fold in carrots and raisins with water; spoon into greased or sprayed muffin tins. Bake at 400° for 15 to 18 minutes. Makes 12 large muffins.

Apple Oatmeal Muffins

1 egg	1 C. oatmeal
¾ C. milk	1/3 C. sugar
1 C. raisins	3 tsp. baking powder
1 C. chopped apples	1 tsp. salt
½ C. oil	1 tsp. nutmeg
1 C. all-purpose flour	2 tsp. cinnamon

Beat egg and stir in remaining ingredients, mixing just to moisten. Pour into 12 greased muffin cups until ¾ full. Bake at 400° for 15 to 20 minutes. Serve cool or hot with butter.

55

APPLE MUFFINS

2 C. flour	1 C. oil
2 tsp. cinnamon	1 C. sugar
1 tsp. baking soda	1 tsp. vanilla
½ tsp. salt	4 C. chopped apples
2 eggs (beat until foamy)	1 C. chopped nuts

Mix all ingredients except apples. After mixture is smooth, add chopped apples and nuts. Blend well. Fill greased muffin tin indentations 2/3 full. Bake at 350˚ for 15 minutes. Makes 24 muffins.

APPLE FRITTERS

¼ C. sugar
2 eggs
1 C. flour
2 tsp. baking powder

½ tsp. salt
Milk
1-2 chopped apples

Mix sugar, eggs, flour, baking powder and salt. Add enough milk to keep a thick batter. Add chopped apples. Drop fritters onto hot skillet. (350° if electric skillet is used.) Brown and turn. Serve warm with syrup or honey.

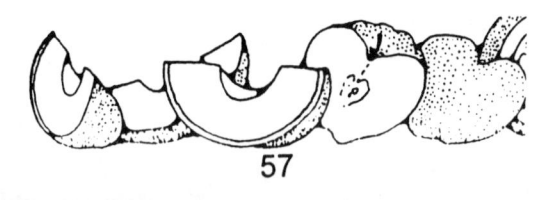

57

BAKED APPLE DOUGHNUTS

3 C. flour
3½ tsp. baking powder
1 tsp. salt
1 tsp. nutmeg
1 C. sugar
⅔ C. shortening

2 eggs (beaten)
½ C. milk
1 C. grated apples
1 C. butter (melted)
⅔ C. sugar
2 tsp. cinnamon

Combine flour, baking powder, salt, nutmeg, and 1 C. sugar. Cut in shortening. Combine eggs, milk and apples. Add to dry ingredients. Mix well. Fill greased muffin tins ⅔ full. Bake at 350° 20 minutes. While doughnuts are still warm, dip in butter then roll in mixture of sugar and cinnamon.

CRISP

APPLE OATMEAL CRISP

4 C. sliced peeled apples
2 T. lemon juice
1/2 C. packed brown sugar
1/2 C. uncooked quick oatmeal
1/4 C. flour

1/4 C. margarine
1 tsp. cinnamon
1/2 tsp. salt
1/8 tsp. ground nutmeg

Place apples in 1-qt. casserole. Sprinkle with lemon juice. Microwave on high until apples are tender-crisp, 2 1/2-4 minutes. Set aside. Combine remaining ingredients in small bowl. Microwave on high until hot and bubbly, 1 1/2-3 1/2 minutes, stirring after half the cooking time. Spread over apples. Microwave on high intil apples are tender and topping is bubbly, 4-6 minutes.

EASY APPLE CRISP

1 C. brown sugar
1 C. quick oatmeal
1 C. oleo
1 C. flour

Apples (sliced)
1 tsp. flour
1 tsp. sugar

Slice a good layer of apples in pan, sprinkle some white sugar and flour on top of apples. Then the layer of brown sugar, oatmeal, oleo and flour on top.

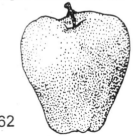

APPLE CRISP, MICROWAVE

4 or 5 C. sliced apples
1 T. flour

1/2 C. sugar

TOPPING:
3/4 C. brown sugar
1/3 C. butter
1/2 C. oatmeal
3/4 C. flour

1/2 tsp. soda
1/2 tsp. salt
1 tsp. cinnamon

Mix apples, flour, and sugar together; place in an 8 x 8-inch baking dish. Mix together brown sugar, butter, flour, oatmeal, soda, salt, and cinnamon and sprinkle over apple mixture. Bake at 350° for 30 minutes or microwave on high setting for 16-18 minutes.

Apple Crisp

1 C. flour
1 C. sugar
¾ tsp. baking powder
¼ tsp. salt

1 egg
Sliced apples
3 T. margarine
Cinnamon

Mix flour, sugar, baking powder, and salt. Beat egg. Cut into mixture until crumbly. Pour over top of sliced apples in square pan. Melt margarine and pour over top. Sprinkle with cinnamon. Bake at 350° for 35 to 40 minutes.

M-m-m APPLE CRISP

4 C. sliced apples
1 C. flour
3/4 C. brown sugar (packed)

1 T. cinnamon
1 T. nutmeg
1/2 C. butter or margarine

Put apples into a buttered 1 1/2-quart baking dish or pan. Blend flour, sugar, cinnamon, nutmeg, and margarine. Sprinkle over apples. May sprinkle sugar and cinnamon between layers of apples. Bake for 30 to 35 minutes until apples are tender and topping is crusty and brown. M-m-m good!

65

APPLE CRISP

1 C. sugar   ½ C. oleo
¾ C. flour   6 apples (peeled)

Slice apples into buttered 8x8-inch pan. Sprinkle with cinnamon and ¼ C. sugar. Cut oleo into sugar and flour; spread over apples. Bake at 350° for 45 minutes to 1 hour.

APPLE-OAT CRISP

1 qt. sliced apples (peeled and
        sweetened to taste)
2/3 C. brown sugar
1/2 C. flour

1/2 C. oats
3/4 tsp. cinnamon
3/4 tsp. nutmeg
1/3 stick butter or oleo

Pour the sweetened apples into a pan about 8-inches square. Mix all other ingredients together and pour over apples. Bake about 30-35 minutes at 350°.

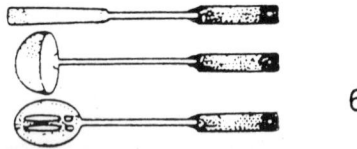

67

MOM'S APPLE CRISP

8 apples (sliced)   ¾ C. flour
1 tsp. cinnamon   4 T. butter
½ C. water

Butter baking dish. Fill with apples, cinnamon and water. Mix remaining ingredients thoroughly. Spread over apples and bake until apples are done. Bake at 375° for 45 minutes.

LOTS OF APPLE CRISP

12-16 apples (pared and sliced)
2 C. sugar
1 tsp. cinnamon
Dash of salt

4 T. flour
½ tsp. nutmeg
½ C. water

TOPPING:
1 C. flour
½ C. margarine (melted)
½ C. nuts

⅔ C. sugar
½ C. coconut

Place apples in a 9x13-inch buttered dish. Mix sugar, cinnamon, salt, flour and nutmeg. Sprinkle over apples. Drizzle water over apples.

For Topping: Mix all ingredients together and spread over apples. Bake at 350° for 50 minutes or until apples are done.

QUICK APPLESAUCE CRISP

2 C. applesauce
½ C. raisins
½ C. light brown sugar

½ C. chopped walnuts
½ tsp. cinnamon
¼ tsp. nutmeg

TOPPING:
½ C. sugar
¼ C. butter

1 C. biscuit mix

Preheat oven to 400°. Combine all of the ingredients except those for the topping and put in a 9-inch pie plate. Mix the topping ingredients using 2 knives or pastry blender, until it is like cornmeal. Then sprinkle this over the applesauce mixture. Bake 30 minutes in moderate oven. Serve warm or cold, plain, or with whipped cream.

MICROWAVE APPLE CRISP

¾ C. oats
1 C. flour
1 C. brown sugar
5 C. sliced apples

½ tsp. salt
1 tsp. cinnamon
½ C. margarine

Mix dry ingredients, cut in ½ C. margarine with pastry blender. Spread this over 5 C. sliced apples in an 8x8-inch glass dish. Cook on full power 15 minutes. Turn every 2 minutes.

71

APPLE-MALLOW CRISP

4½ C. sliced apples
2 T. sugar
1 tsp. cinnamon
¼ tsp. nutmeg
2 tsp. lemon juice

8 marshmallows (quartered)
½ C. flour
¼ C. brown sugar (firmly packed)
½ tsp. salt
¼ C. butter or oleo

Combine apples, sugar, cinnamon, nutmeg, lemon juice and ¾ of the marshmallows. Butter a 1½-qt. baking dish. Spread apple mixture in dish in even layers. Combine flour, brown sugar and salt. Cut in butter until mixture is crumbly. Sprinkle over top of apples in baking dish. Dot with reserved marshmallows. Bake in 350° oven for 30-40 minutes until apples are tender and top crisp.

CRISP

3-4 medium sized apples
½ tsp. cinnamon
½ C. brown sugar
½ C. oatmeal

½ C. sugar
½ C. butter or margarine
½ C. flour

Slice apples into 8 × 8-inch buttered pan. Sprinkle with sugar and cinnamon. Place over low heat and partially cook while mixing topping. Mix remaining ingredients together and spread over apples. Bake at 350° for about 25 minutes or until browned. This is easy to remember, because everything is measured by halves.

73

QUICK APPLE OR RHUBARB CRISP

5 or 6 apples, sliced (or about 3 C. diced rhubarb)

1 1/2 C. sugar for apples (or 2 C. sugar for rhubarb)

1/2 tsp. salt

1/2 C. water for apples

cinnamon to taste

1 stick of margarine

2 C. flour

1/2 C. sugar

Slice apples, (or cut up rhubarb,) and place in the bottom of an 8-inch square baking dish. Fill dish half full with fruit. Sprinkle sugar and salt over fruit. Add water if using apples (no water with rhubarb.) Sprinkle cinnamon to taste over top. In a bowl, cut margarine into flour and mix in the 1/2 C. sugar until mixture is in small crumbly bits. Sprinkle generously over fruit and pat down. Bake 40 minutes in 350˚ oven.

WARM APPLE CRISP

6 C. apples (thinly sliced & peeled)
⅓ C. sugar
1 tsp. cinnamon
½ tsp. salt

¾ C. sugar
½ C. flour
⅓ C. butter or margarine
2 T. butter or margarine (melted)

Mix together apples, sugar, cinnamon, salt and melted butter. Place in greased 8-inch square baking dish; set aside. Combine ¾ C. sugar and flour. Cut in butter until crumbly. Sprinkle over apples. Bake at 375° for 45 minutes or until apples are tender. Serve warm with drops of whipped topping. Makes 8 servings.

CAKES

DICED APPLE CAKE

4½ T. butter or oleo
1½ C. sugar
1 egg
1½ C. flour
1½ tsp. soda
1½ tsp. vanilla

¾ tsp. salt
4½ C. diced apples
½ tsp. cinnamon
½ tsp. nutmeg
½ C. nuts

Cream butter and sugar; add egg. Add flour, soda, salt, spices and vanilla. Fold in apples and nuts. Batter will be very thick. Bake in a 9x13-inch pan at 350° for 35 minutes. Serve with whipped cream or ice cream.

APPLE CHOPPED NUT CAKE

2 eggs
2 C. sugar
2 tsp. soda
2 tsp. cinnamon
1 tsp. vanilla

2 C. flour
4 C. diced apples
½ C. oil
1 C. chopped nuts

Chop apples and set aside. Mix eggs, sugar and oil. Add dry ingredients, then apples and nuts. Batter will be thick. Pour in 9x13-inch pan and bake at 350° for 35 to 45 minutes. Frost with cream cheese frosting, Cool Whip or a topping of 1 C. brown sugar, ½ stick of margarine and 2 T. flour which you spread over the batter before baking.

APPLE CAKE

1 C. milk
2 eggs
1½ C. sugar
1 tsp. vanilla
2 C. flour
4 tsp. baking powder

⅔ tsp. salt
5-6 sliced apples
1-1½ C. brown sugar
1 tsp. cinnamon
1/8 lb. butter

Grease 9x13-inch pan. Mix eggs, sugar, milk, and vanilla together. Mix flour, baking powder, and salt together. Blend well, pour into greased cake pan. Pour apples over top and a little cinnamon. Then top with 1-1½ C. brown sugar and small slices of butter. Bake at 350° for 45 minutes. (1 - 2½x2½-inch slice = 213 calories; no oil.)

RAW APPLE CAKE

1 C. sugar
½ C. shortening
1 egg
1½ C. flour

1 tsp. baking soda
1 tsp. salt
Cinnamon to taste
2 C. chopped raw apples

TOPPING:
½ C. brown sugar
1 T. butter

½ C. milk

Cream together sugar and shortening; add egg. Mix together dry ingredients then add to creamed mixture plus the apples. Pour into 9 or 10-inch non-metalic baking dishes. Micro-cook on roast 14 minutes. Brown on level for 5 minutes. Combine all three topping ingredients and spread on hot cake.

SHREDDED RAW APPLE CAKE

1/2 C. Butter
1 C. sugar
2 T. dry, unsweetened cocoa
2 eggs (beaten)
1 1/2 C. flour
1/4 tsp. baking powder

1 tsp. baking soda
1/2 tsp. salt
1 tsp. cinnamon
1/2 tsp. cloves
1/2 C. water
1 C. peeled, shredded raw apples

Cream together butter, sugar, and cocoa. Add eggs. Mix dry ingredients in a small bowl. Add mixture to butter mixture alternately with water, beating after each addition. Fold in shredded apple. Grease and flour an 8 x 8-inch cake pan. Pour in batter. Bake at 350° for about 45 minutes, until cake bounces back from touch.

83

RAW APPLE COCONUT CAKE

		For Topping
2 C. chopped raw apple	2 1/2 C. flour	1 stick margarine
1 C. brown sugar	1/2 tsp. salt	3/4 C. brown sugar
1 C. white sugar	1 tsp. soda	1 C. flake coconut
1 stick Margarine (softened)	1 tsp. vanilla	1/2 C. chopped nuts
2 eggs (beaten)	1/2 C. milk	

Cream sugar and margarine. Add eggs and beat well. Sift flour, salt, and soda together. Stir the dry ingredients into the mixture alternately with the milk and vanilla. Fold in the nuts and pour into a 9 x 13-inch baking dish.

Topping: Blend margarine, brown sugar, coconut, and nuts until well mixed and crumbly. Sprinkle over batter. Bake at 350° for about 55 minutes.

RAW APPLE CAKE

4 C. apples (peeled and sliced)   2 C. sugar

DRY INGREDIENTS:
2 C. flour   2 tsp. cinnamon
1½ tsp. soda   1 tsp. salt

WET INGREDIENTS:
2 eggs   2 tsp. vanilla
¾ C. salad oil   1 C. chopped nuts

Pour sugar over apples and let stand ½ hour. Combine dry ingredients. Then combine eggs, oil, and vanilla and add to dry ingredients with a fork. Mix in apples and add nuts. Beat to batter consistency (wet). Grease and flour 9x13-inch pan. Bake 40-45 minutes in 350° oven.

RAW APPLE CAKE

8 medium apples (chopped fine)
2 C. sugar
½ C. margarine
2 eggs

1 tsp. cinnamon
2 C. flour
2 tsp. baking soda
1 C. nuts

Mix ingredients and spread in 9x13-inch pan. Spray with Pam. Bake at 350° for 25 minutes.

TOPPING:
¼ C. margarine
1 C. brown sugar

1 C. water
2 T. cornstarch

Mix and boil ingredients until thick. Spread on cake after cake is cooled.

RAW APPLE CAKE

3 C. chopped apples
2 C. sugar
3 C. flour
1 tsp. cinnamon
2 eggs

1 tsp. salt
1 tsp. soda
1 tsp. vanilla
1 1/2 C. oil
1/2 C. nuts of choice

Cream eggs, oil, and sugar together. Add remaining ingredients and stir. Pour into greased 9 x 13- inch baking dish and bake 35 - 45 minutes at 350°

87

RAW APPLE CAKE WITH SOUR CREAM TOPPING

1 C. nuts	1 tsp. cinnamon
2 C. diced apples	1 tsp. soda
1 C. oil	½ tsp. nutmeg
2 C. sugar	½ tsp. salt
1 tsp. vanilla	12 oz. jar Smucker's caramel sauce
2 eggs (beaten)	½ C. sour cream
2 C. flour	

Mix together nuts, sugar, diced apples, oil, vanilla and eggs. Sift together flour, soda, cinnamon, nutmeg and salt. Mix into first mixture. Bake at 350° for 1 hour. Serves 12 to 15. Mix together caramel sauce and sour cream for topping. Serve with Cool Whip and garnish with maraschino cherries.

Applesauce Cake

⅔ C. shortening
2 ⅔ C. sugar
2 eggs
⅔ C. water
3 ⅓ C. flour
½ tsp. baking powder
2 tsp. soda

1 tsp. salt
1 tsp. cinnamon
1 tsp. cloves
2 C. thick applesauce
⅔ C. chopped nuts
1 C. raisins

Cream shortening and sugar; add eggs and water. In a separate bowl mix flour, baking powder, soda, salt, cinnamon and cloves. Slowly add dry ingredients to creamed mixture. Add applesauce, nuts and raisins. (I like to use ½ C. raisins and ½ C. dried apricots.) Bake at 350° until a toothpick comes out clean. This cake keeps well. It makes a nice Christmas cake for gifts.

HOLIDAY APPLESAUCE CAKE

1 C. shortening	1 tsp. baking powder
2 C. sugar	1 tsp. cinnamon
2 C. applesauce	1/2 tsp. salt
1 egg	1 C. broken nuts
4 C. flour	2 C. orange slice candy
1 tsp. (rounded) baking soda	(cut up)
mixed in 1/4 C. hot water	

Cream shortening and sugar. Add applesauce, egg and soda. Mix dry ingredients. Pour some of the dry mixture over nuts and candy and mix well. Add to first mixture. Bake 1 hour in greased 9x13-inch pan at 325 . Nice holiday cake!

APPLESAUCE RAISIN CAKE

1 C. shortening
2 C. sugar
2 eggs
2 C. applesauce
½ tsp. salt
1 tsp. cloves

2 tsp. cinnamon
2 tsp. soda
2½ C. flour
1 C. nuts
1 C. raisins (which have been cooked a few minutes)

Cream shortening and sugar; add eggs. Alternately add remaining ingredients. Bake at 350° for 50 minutes. (I use a powdered sugar frosting or cream cheese frosting.)

91

SPICY APPLESAUCE CAKE

2 C. sugar
½ C. shortening
2 C. applesauce
3 C. flour
2 C. raisins
1 C. nuts (optional)
2 eggs

2 tsp. cinnamon
1 tsp. ginger
1 tsp. allspice
½ tsp. mace
2 tsp. soda
½ tsp. salt

Mix and sift together flour, soda, salt and spices. Cream sugar and shortening. Add eggs and applesauce. Mix with dry ingredients and raisins; beat well. Pour into 9x13-inch pan and bake in moderate (350°) oven. Frost with favorite icing.

APPLE CAKE WITH FROSTING

1 ½ C. oil
3 C. flour
1 tsp. baking soda
1 tsp. salt

1 tsp. cinnamon
3 C. apples
1 C. nuts

FROSTING:
1 (8 oz.) pkg. cream cheese
1 ½ C. powdered sugar

2 tsp. vanilla
1 tsp. cinnamon

Mix together two beaten eggs and 2 C. sugar. Add oil, flour, soda, salt and cinnamon. Stir in 3 C. apples and 1 C. nuts. Bake at 350° for 35-40 minutes. When cake is cooled, frost with cream cheese frosting.

93

FRESH APPLE SHEET CAKE

1½ C. sugar
2 eggs
1 tsp. cinnamon
¼ tsp. salt
¼ tsp. nutmeg

3 C. diced fresh apples
1 tsp. soda
½ C. nutmeats
1½ C. flour
½ C. shortening

Cream sugar and shortening. Add eggs and beat well. Sift all dry ingredients, then add them to the creamed mixture. Fold in apples and nuts. Bake 45 minutes at 350°. Top with a caramel frosting or eat warm, topped with whipped cream. Makes a 9x13-inch sheet cake.

APPLESAUCE FRUIT CAKE

3 C. applesauce
1 C. shortening
2 C. sugar
1 lb. dates (chopped)
1 lb. raisins (light or dark)
1 lb. nuts (chopped)
½ lb. candied cherries (quartered)
½ lb. candied pineapple (chopped)

½ lb. candied citron
   (finely chopped)
4½ C. flour (sifted)
4 tsp. soda
1 tsp. nutmeg
2½ tsp. cinnamon
½ tsp. ground cloves
1 tsp. salt

Combine applesauce, shortening and sugar in sauce pan, bring to a boil and simmer for 5 minutes, stirring occasionally. Allow to cool. Mix fruits and nuts together in a large bowl. Sift the flour, spices and soda over the fruit and nuts and mix well. Stir the cooled applesauce mixture into this. Turn mixture into pans filling each about

(more)

(continued)

¾ full. Bake in a slow oven at 250° for about 2 hours. When cakes are as brown as you want them to be, cover with brown paper so the baking can continue without any more browning. Before serving combine ½ C. light corn syrup and ½ C. water, bring to boil. Cool to lukewarm and pour over the cold cake for a shiny glaze.

FRESH APPLE WALNUT CAKE

1 C. butter or margarine
2 C. sugar
3 eggs
3 C. flour (sifted)
1 ½ tsp. baking soda
½ tsp. salt

1 tsp. cinnamon
¼ tsp. mace
1 tsp. vanilla
3 C. chopped apples
2 C. chopped walnuts

Cream butter and sugar until fluffy; add eggs one at a time, beating well after each. Mix and sift flour, baking soda, salt, cinnamon and mace. Add gradually. Stir in vanilla, apples and walnuts. Batter will be stiff. Spoon into greased and floured 10-inch tube pan. Bake in 325° oven for 1½ hours. Let cool in pan 10 minutes. Remove and let cool on rack. Top with whipped topping. Cuts 14-16.

APPLESAUCE CAKE

Dry Ingredients:
1½ C. flour
1 c. sugar
1 tsp. soda

½ tsp. salt
1 tsp. cinnamon
½ tsp. nutmeg

Wet Ingredients:
1 T. vinegar
6 T. margarine

¾ C. applesauce
¼ - ½ C. cold water

Mix dry ingredients in baking pan used to bake the cake in. Add wet ingredients, stir until well mixed. Bake in 350° oven for 30-35 minutes.

FRESH APPLE CAKE

1¼ C. oil
2 C. sugar
3 eggs (well beaten)
3-4 app es (chopped)
3 C. flour

1 tsp. soda
2 tsp. vanilla
1 tsp. cinnamon
1 tsp. allspice

Combine oil, eggs, sugar, then add flour, soda. Stir well. Add vanilla and spices. Then apples. Pour in pan and place in cold oven. Set oven at 350° and bake 45 minutes to 1 hour.

Apple Bundt Cake

2 eggs
2 C. sugar
½ C. oil
2 tsp. baking soda
½ tsp. salt
1 C. nuts (chopped)

2 C. all-purpose flour (sifted)
1 tsp. cinnamon
4 C. peeled & diced apples
½ C. chopped nuts
½ tsp. vanilla

Beat eggs; add sugar and mix well. Add oil and sifted dry ingredients and blend thoroughly. Stir in diced apples, nuts, and vanilla. Batter will be very thick. Spoon into a greased and floured bundt pan. Bake at 350° for 1 hour. Cool in pan for 10 to 15 minutes. Turn onto plate. You may drizzle powdered sugar frosting over it when removed from pan. This is a very moist, delicious cake. It could also be served with Cool Whip or ice cream.

Apple Nut Cake

1 C. cooking oil	1 tsp. soda
2 C. sugar	1 tsp. salt
3 eggs	3 C. diced apples
2 tsp. vanilla	1 C. chopped nuts
3 C. flour	

Mix together oil, sugar, eggs, and vanilla. Add flour, soda, salt, apples, and nuts. Bake at 350° for 1 hour in angel food cake pan. Remove from pan when cool.

TOPPING FOR APPLE NUT CAKE:
1 stick oleo
1 C. brown sugar   ¼ C. milk

Cook for 3 to 4 minutes and pour over cake.

Apple Cake

4 C. chopped apples
2 C. sugar
2 beaten eggs
2 C all-purpose flour
2 tsp. baking soda
3 tsp. cinnamon
1 tsp. salt

1 C. brown sugar
1 C. granulated sugar
6 T. all-purpose flour
2 C. water
½ C. margarine or butter
1 tsp. vanilla
1 C. walnuts (chopped)

Mix apples and 2 C. sugar and let stand for 1 hour or longer. Add eggs, 2 C. flour, soda, cinnamon, salt, and nuts. Mix and put into 9x13-inch greased pan. Bake at 350° for 45 minutes.

(more)

(continued)

For Topping: During last 15 to 20 minutes of baking time, mix together brown sugar, granulated sugar, 6 T. flour, and water. Bring to a boil, stirring often. Turn down heat and simmer for 15 minutes. Remove from heat and add butter, vanilla, and nuts. Pour over the cake while hot. Serve warm or cold.

104

Grandma's Apple Cake

1 stick butter or margarine
1/2 C. sugar
2-3 eggs
Salt
1 3/4 C. flour

2 tsp. baking powder
1-4 T. milk
Lemon flavoring(optional)
1-2 apples

Smooth butter and add slowly to sugar, eggs, and spices. Mix flour
and baking powder; add tablespoon by tablespoon to the mixture. If
dough is to stiff, add milk. Put in greased baking tin and level. Peel
apple, quarter it and cut apple quarter, not through horizontal and
vertical and put them in the dough. Bake at 325° for 40-50 minutes.
Sieve powder suger on the cold cake.

SWEETENED APPLESAUCE CAKE

½ C. shortening
1 C. sugar
2 eggs (beaten)
1 ½ C. sweetened applesauce
2 C. all-purpose flour
1 tsp. baking soda

½ tsp. salt
1 tsp. cinnamon
½ tsp. cloves
½ tsp. nutmeg
1 C. raisins
1 tsp. vanilla

Cream shortening and sugar together. Add beaten eggs. Add applesauce and vanilla. Sift together flour, soda, salt, cinnamon, cloves, and nutmeg. Add to applesauce mixture. Put into a greased 9x13-inch pan. Bake at 350° for 40 to 45 minutes.

APPLESAUCE CHIP CAKE

2 C. flour
2 C. brown sugar
1 C. softened margarine
1 C. sweetened applesauce
1 egg
1/2 tsp. salt

1 1/2 tsp. cinnamon
1 tsp. baking soda
2 T. boiling water
1 C. coconut
1/2 C. chopped nuts
1/2 C. chocalate chips

Mix flour, brown sugar, and softened margarine. Reserve 1 C. for topping. To the remainder add the applesauce, egg, salt, cinnamon, and baking soda, dissolve in boiling water. Mix together and pour into a 9 x 12-inch greased pan. To the reserved mixture, add the coconut, nuts, and chocolate chips. Sprinkle over cake. Bake at 325° for 50 minutes.

APPLE PUDDING CAKE

1/2 C. melted shortening
2 C. sugar
2 eggs (beaten)
2 C. flour

TOPPING:
1/2 C. brown sugar
1 tsp. cinnamon

2 tsp. soda
1/2 tsp. salt
4 C. raw chopped apple

2 T. butter
1 C. nutmeats

Cream melted shortening and sugar together. Add beaten eggs. Add flour, soda, salt, and raw chopped apples. Place in a large cake pan. Simply mix topping ingredients and top cake. Bake at 350° for 45 min.

APPLE SPICE CAKE

1 C. sugar
1 egg (beaten)
½ C. oleo
½ C. cold coffee
1 C. chopped peeled raw apples

1 tsp. cinnamon
1 tsp. cloves
Scant tsp. soda
1½ C. sifted flour
Brown sugar & nuts

Cream sugar and oleo; add egg. Add remaining ingredients, except apples. Stir and add apples. Sprinkle with brown sugar and nuts. Pour Into 11x7½-inch pan. Bake at 375° for 40 minutes.

109

110

PIES

SWEDISH APPLE PIE

Apples
1 T. sugar
1 tsp. cinnamon
¾ C. melted butter
1 C. sugar

1 C. flour
1 egg
Pinch of salt
¼ C. nuts (optional)

For 9x9-inch pan, fill ⅔ full of apples. Sprinkle sugar and cinnamon on top. Combine remaining ingredients in bowl and pour over apples. Bake at 350° for 45 minutes
Note: Peaches or most any fruit can be substituted for apples.

113

DUTCH APPLE PIE

Plain pastry for 1 crust
6 medium-sized apples
3 T. flour
1 C. sugar

¼ tsp. cloves
1 C. sour cream
½ tsp. cinnamon
1½ T. sugar

Roll out crust to about 1/8-inch thick and line pie pan. Flute edges. **Pare, core, and slice** apples medium thin. Fill pastry shell. Mix flour, sugar, and cloves together. Add sour cream, and mix thoroughly. Pour over apples. Sprinkle cinnamon and 1½ T. sugar over top. Bake in a hot oven for 10 minutes, then reduce heat to moderate and finish baking. Serve warm or chilled.

Pie

1 egg
¾ C. sugar
¾ C. flour
1/8 tsp. salt

1¼ tsp. baking powder
1 C. pared, diced apples
1 C. chopped nuts
1 tsp. vanilla flavoring

Beat egg and stir in sugar. Add flour, salt, and baking powder; stir about 1 minute. Add remaining ingredients. Spread mixture into a greased pie pan. Bake at 350° for 30 to 35 minutes. Top with ice cream or whipping cream.

Apple Betty Pie

4 C. sliced pared tart apples
¼ C. orange juice
1 C. sugar
¾ C. flour

½ tsp. cinnamon
¼ tsp. nutmeg
½ C. butter

Mound apples in buttered 9-inch pie plate and sprinkle with orange juice.

For Topping: Combine sugar, flour, spices, and dash of salt. Cut in butter until mixture is crumbly, then scatter over apples. Bake at 375° for 45 minutes or until apples are done and topping is crisp. Serve warm with cream or ice cream.

Apple Crumb Pie

4 large tart apples
1 unbaked pastry shell
1 C. sugar

1 tsp. cinnamon
¾ C. flour (scant)
⅓ C. butter

Peel apples, slice, and arrange in unbaked pastry shell. Sprinkle with ½ C. sugar, mixed with cinnamon. Sift remaining ½ C. sugar with flour. Cut butter into sugar and flour until very crumbly. Sprinkle over apples. Bake in hot oven at 450° about 10 minutes. Reduce heat to 350° and bake for 30 minutes, until apples are tender.

Uncle Hursh's Variation: Use apple pie spice instead of cinnamon and add ½ to ¾ C. dark raisins.

APPLE CRUMB PIE

4 large tart apples
1 C. sugar
1 tsp. cinnamon

¾ C. flour
⅓ C. butter

Pare apples, cut in eighths and arrange in a 9-inch pastry-lined pie pan. Sprinkle with ½ C. sugar mixed with cinnamon. Sift remaining ½ C. sugar with flour. Cut in butter until crumbly. Sprinkle over apples. Bake in hot oven (450°) for 10 minutes. Decrease heat to 350° about 40 minutes or until apples are tender.

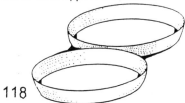

118

APPLE PIE IN A JAR

Apples

Peel and slice apples. Fill quart jars tightly, cover with syrup. Process 20 minutes in water bath.

SYRUP:

4 ½ C. sugar

1 C. cornstarch

2 tsp. cinnamon

¼ tsp. nutmeg

1 tsp. salt

10 C. water

Cook syrup until thick and bubbly. Add 3 T. lemon juice.

ONE CRUST APPLE PIE

4-5 apples (chopped fine)
1 C. sugar
1 C. milk

⅓ C. flour
1 unbaked pie shell

Mix well and put into unbaked pie shell. Sprinkle cinnamon and bits of butter on top. Bake in a moderate oven.

DUTCH APPLE PIE WITH BREAD CRUMBS

1 unbaked pie shell   Sugar
Apples   Cinnamon
Sweet cream   Bread crumbs

After lining the pie tin with a nice rich crust, cover the bottom with bread crumbs; then pare and core tart apples. Cut them into eighths and place side by side on the bread crumbs until the pan is full. Cover with sweet cream, sugar enough to sweeten, and flavor with cinnamon. Bake without an upper crust at 350° for 1 hour or until apples are done.

SOUR CREAM APPLE PIE

1½ lbs. tart apples - peeled and
  sliced lengthwise
⅓ C. flour

¼ tsp. cinnamon
½ C. sour cream or top milk
Pie crust for one crust pie

Arrange slices of apples, overlapping each other in rows, filling pie crust. Mix together sugar, flour and cinnamon. Sprinkle over the apples; add sour cream. Make a lattice top for the pie from the remaining dough. Bake in a hot oven, 400°, for 10-15 minutes. Reduce heat to 350° and continue to bake about 40 minutes or until apples are tender and crust is brown.

OUR FAVORITE APPLE PIE

7 tart apples
¾ C. sugar
2 T. flour
1 tsp. cinnamon

Dash nutmeg
Dash salt
Pastry for 2-crust 9-inch pie
2 T. butter or margarine

Pare apples and slice thin. Combine sugar, flour, spices and salt. Mix with apples. Line 9-inch pie plate with pastry, fill with apple mixture; dot with butter. Adjust top crust; sprinkle with sugar for sparkle. Bake in hot oven (400°) for 50 minutes.

CRUSTLESS APPLE PIE

¾ C. sugar
1 C. water
2 T. cinnamon candies
1 ½ C. diced apples

1 C. prepared biscuit mix
2 T. sugar
½ C. cream
1 T. butter

Combine the ¾ C. sugar and water. Add the red hots and a few drops red food coloring, if desired. Cook 5 minutes. Add diced apples and cook until tender. Mix biscuit mix with the 2 T. sugar and the cream. Drop by spoonfuls.

EASY STREUSEL APPLE PIE

1½ C. flour	½ C. salad oil
1½ tsp. sugar	2 T. cold milk
1 tsp. salt	apples

Sift flour, sugar, and salt into a 9-inch pie pan. Whip together oil and milk; pour over flour mixture and mix until dampened. Press with fingers to line bottom of pan; press dough up to line sides and partly cover rim. Be sure dough is pressed to uniform thickness. Flute dough lightly with fingers or press with fork. Do not use high fluted edge.

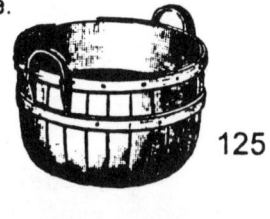

(more)

125

(continued)

FILLING:

6-7 C. apples (sliced) ½ tsp. cinnamon
¾ C. sugar

Mix sugar and cinnamon, gently. Mix in with apples. Heap in pastry lined pan. Sprinkle with topping: ½ C. butter, ½ tsp. cinnamon, ½ C. brown sugar, 1 C. flour. Cream together sugar, butter, and cinnamon. Cut in flour and sprinkle over apples. Bake in hot oven (400°) for 15 minutes; reduce heat to moderate (350°) and bake until crust is brown and apples are done (30-40 minutes).

APPLE PIE FILLING

7 1/2 qt. sliced apples
3 1/2 C. sugar
  1/2 C. cornstarch

1/2 tsp. pickling salt
1 1/2 C. corn syrup
1/2 C. lemon juice

Combine sugar, cornstarch, cinnamon, and salt; mix. Add corn syrup and lernon juice. Bring to a boil over medium heat. Stir and boil for 2 minutes. Increase heat and add aplles. Boil 3 minutes. Remove apples from syrup. Pack apples in jars. Bring syrup to boil and pour over apples. Water bath for 20 minutes.

HOME CANNED APPLE PIE FILLING

8-9 lbs. firm apples
10 C. water
4½ C. sugar
1 C. quick tapioca
2-3 drops yellow food color

1 tsp. salt
2 tsp. cinnamon
¼ tsp. nutmeg
3 T. bottled lemon juice

Core, peel, quarter, slice apples in salt water solution. Combine water, sugar, tapioca, cinnamon, salt, nutmeg and lemon juice in 12-qt. kettle. Cook and stir on medium heat until bubbly and thickened. Boil 2-3 minutes more. Add sliced apples, return to boil for 1 minute more. Spoon into sterile jars to 1-inch from top. Wipe edge, adjust lids, place in water bath and process 25 minutes after all returns to boil. Do not use windfall apples.

APPLE PIE

1 egg
½ tsp. vanilla
¾ C. sugar

½ C. flour
½ tsp. baking powder
¼ tsp. salt

In a bowl beat egg and vanilla. In another bowl mix sugar, flour, baking powder, and salt. Stir into beaten egg mixture. Add 1 C. chopped apples and ½ C. nuts (chopped). Mix and pour into a greased 10-inch pie pan (no crust) and bake at 350° for 30 minutes. When cool, cut in wedges and serve as usual.

COOKIES

APPLESAUCE-DATE COOKIES

½ C. butter
1 C. sugar
1 C. applesauce
1 C. chopped dates
1 beaten egg
2 C. flour

½ tsp. cinnamon
½ tsp. nutmeg
¼ tsp. cloves
¼ tsp. salt
1 tsp. baking soda

Mix chopped dates and applesauce; set on counter overnight. In the morning, cream the sugar, and butter. Add the beaten egg, and the flour which has been blended with the remaining ingredients. Fold in the applesauce-date mixture. Drop on greased sheet. Bake at 350° for 9 to 10 minutes. Do not overbake.

133

BRAN APPLESAUCE COOKIES

1¾ C. flour
1 tsp. cinnamon
½ tsp. nutmeg
½ tsp. cloves
½ tsp. salt
1 tsp. soda

1 C. sugar
½ C. shortening
1 egg (beaten)
1 C. applesauce
1 C. raisins
1 C. shredded All-Bran

Cream sugar and shortening. Add egg and applesauce and then dry ingredients. Pour into greased pan, 8x13-inch. Bake at 375° for 25-30 minutes. Good frosted too!

APPLEDOODLES

2⅔ C. flour
2 tsp. baking powder
¼ tsp. salt
½ tsp. cinnamon
½ tsp. nutmeg
½ C. butter (softened)
½ C. sugar

½ C. brown sugar
2 eggs (slightly beaten)
1 tsp. vanilla
1 C. apple (shredded)
2 T. sugar
1 tsp. cinnamon

Stir together flour, baking powder, salt, cinnamon and nutmeg. Cream together butter, ½ C. white and ½ C. brown sugar. Add eggs and vanilla; mix thoroughly. Combine flour mixture and sugar mixture. Add apple. Combine remaining sugar and cinnamon. Shape dough into balls with teaspoons and roll in cinnamon-sugar. Bake on greased cookie sheet in preheated 350° oven for 12-15 minutes or until brown. Makes about 4 dozen cookies.

135

APPLE HERMITS

½ C. oleo
1 C. brown sugar
2 eggs
½ C. nuts
1 C. raisins
½ C. quick rolled oats

1 C. chopped apples
½ tsp. cinnamon
¾ tsp. baking powder
¼ tsp. soda
1 ¾ T. flour
Pinch of salt

Cream oleo and brown sugar. Add other ingredients and mix well. Drop by teaspoon on cookie sheet. Bake at 325° until nicely brown, 10-12 minutes.

OATMEAL APPLE COOKIES

½ C. shortening
2 well beaten eggs
1 C. brown sugar
¼ C. white sugar
½ C. quick oatmeal
½ tsp. soda

1 C. chopped raw apples
1¾ C. flour
½ tsp. baking powder
½ tsp. cinnamon
¼ tsp. salt
1 C. chopped nuts

Thoroughly cream shortening and sugar. Add eggs, beat well. Add oatmeal, fruit and dry ingredients and nuts. Mix well. Drop by teaspoonful on greased cookie sheet. Bake in 350° oven for 12 minutes. These are good keepers.

138

OTHER DESSERTS

APPLESAUCE BARS

1 C. sugar
½ C. soft margarine
2 C. flour
1 tsp. baking soda
¾ tsp. cinnamon

¼ tsp. nutmeg
1 tsp. vanilla
1½ C. applesauce
1 C. chopped nuts
1 C. raisins

Cream together sugar and margarine. Sift dry ingredients together and add to creamed mixture. Add applesauce, nuts and raisins. Pour into a 15x10x1-inch jelly roll pan. Bake at 350° for 25 minutes. Sprinkle with powdered sugar. Cut into squares after it is cool.

APPLE NUT BARS

1 C. chopped nuts
5 C. sifted flour
1 tsp. allspice
2 C. applesauce
1½ C. oil
2 tsp. vanilla

1 C. chopped raisins or dates
2 tsp. cinnamon
2 tsp. salt
2 C. sugar
2 tsp. baking soda

Mix well and pour into three greased 9 x 13-inch pans. Bake at 350° for 15 to 20 minutes. Ice or glaze with 1 C. powdered sugar and milk.

APPLE CORN FLAKE BARS

CRUST:
2 ½ C. flour
1 C. Crisco
1 T. sugar

1 tsp. salt
1 egg yolk &
enough milk to make ⅔ C.

FILLING:
5 C. apples (sliced)
1 C. sugar
⅔ C. corn flake crumbs

1 T. cinnamon
Dash of salt

Divide dough in half. Roll out half to fit jelly roll pan. Coat apples with sugar, flakes and cinnamon. Put top on and seal, then brush with foamy egg white. Bake at 375° for 40 to 45 minutes. While still warm, frost with powdered sugar frosting. Add a little lemon juice to it if you want.

143

CRUMBLE APPLE BARS

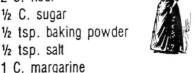

2 C. flour
½ C. sugar
½ tsp. baking powder
½ tsp. salt
1 C. margarine

4 medium apples (sliced, 4 C.)
¼ C. flour
¾ C. sugar
1 tsp. cinnamon

Combine first 4 ingredients. Cut in margarine. Stir in 2 egg yolks. Divide mixture in half. Put half in bottom of a cookie sheet. Combine apples, flour, sugar, and cinnamon. Arrange over crust. Crumble remaining dough over apples. Brush 1 egg white over all. Bake at 350° for 40-45 minutes. Drizzle frosting over the top. Yield: 4 dozen.

APPLE BARS WITH FROSTING

2½ C. flour
¼ tsp. salt
1 C. shortening
1 egg yolk
Milk

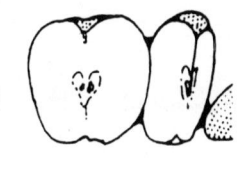

1 C. crushed corn flakes
4 large apples (sliced)
1 C. sugar
1 tsp. cinnamon

(more)

(continued)

Add salt to flour and cut in shortening like pie crust. Beat yolk and add enough milk to egg yolk to make ⅔ cup. Add to dough mixture. Roll out ½ of dough and put in 10x15-inch pan. Cover dough with corn flakes, then with apple slices and sprinkle with sugar and cinnamon mixture over top. Roll out rest of dough and spread over top. Make cuts in top to let out steam. Beat egg white until stiff and brush over top. Bake at 350° for 1 hour. While still warm, frost with 1 C. powdered sugar, 1 T. water and 1 tsp. vanilla.

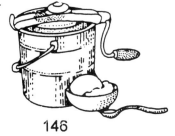

146

APPLE BARS

2½ C. flour
1 tsp. salt
½ C. shortening
½ C. oleo
1 egg yolk
1 C. corn flakes

8-10 apples
1 C. sugar
1 tsp. cinnamon
1 egg white
1 C. powdered sugar
3 or 4 tsp. milk

Combine flour and salt. Cut in shortening and oleo. Beat egg yolk in measuring cup and add enough milk to make ⅔ C. liquid. Mix well and stir into flour mixture. Roll ½ dough into 17x12-inch rectangle. Put into 1x15½x10½-inch baking pan. Crush and sprinkle corn flakes on dough; top with apples. Combine sugar and cinnamon; sprinkle on top. Roll remaining dough and place on top. Seal edges and cut slits in dough. Beat egg white until frothy. Brush on top of crust. Bake at 375° for 50 minutes. Top with powdered sugar frosting.

DEB'S APPLE BARS

2½ C. flour
1 tsp. salt
1 C. shortening (Crisco)
1 egg yolk. add enough milk to
   make ⅔ C.

1 C. crushed corn flakes
8-10 medium apples
1 C. sugar
1 tsp. cinnamon
1 egg white

Cut shortening into flour and salt. Add milk and yolk; blend with fork. Roll ½ dough to fill 10½ x 15½-inch cookie sheet. Sprinkle bottom crust with crushed flakes. Peel and slice apples; place over crust and flakes. Sprinkle with sugar and cinnamon. Roll out other half of dough and place on top; pinch edges. Beat egg whites stiff and brush over crust. Bake at 375° for 35 to 45 minutes. While warm pour frosting over warm crust. For Frosting: Mix 1 T. water, ½ tsp. vanilla and 1 C. powdered sugar.

Apple Pie Bar

PASTRY:

4 1/2 C. flour

1 tsp. baking powder

Mix above and then add:

3 eggs

1 tsp. salt

1 1/2 C. Crisco

1/2-3/4 C. milk

FILLING:

1 1/2 C. sugar

1 T. cinnamon

3 T. flour

Add 10-12 peeled and cut apples

(more)

(continued)

Mix pastry and roll out dough. Place ½ of mixture on large cookie sheet with sides. Mix filling; add peeled and cut apples and pour over crust. Roll out rest of dough and put on top (doesn't matter if you have to piece it). Brush with ¼ C. milk and sugar and cinnamon mixture for brownness. Bake for 50-60 minutes until golden at 350°. Frost with white frosting when done.

Squash and Apple Bake

2 medium butternut squash
2 T. brown sugar
2 T. margarine (melted)

1 T. flour
¼ tsp. nutmeg
2 apples (cored and cut into
½-inch slices)

Cut squash into ½-inch slices. Stir together sugar, butter, flour and nutmeg; set aside. Arrange squash in ungreased 11x7-inch baking dish; top with apple slices. Sprinkle sugar mixture over top; cover with foil. Bake at 350° for about 50 minutes or until squash is tender.

APPLESAUCE BROWNIES

½ C. butter
2 sq. chocolate or 2 T. cocoa
1 C. sugar
2 well-beaten eggs
½ C. applesauce

1 C. flour
½ tsp. soda
½ tsp. salt
1 tsp. vanilla
½ C. nuts

Melt butter and chocolate together. Blend in sugar and and remaining ingredients.
Bake at 350° for 40 minutes. Frost or use powdered sugar.

APPLE CRUNCH

Caramel sauce (at right)
5 C. sliced pared apples
  (about 5 medium)
½ tsp. cinnamon

CARAMEL SAUCE:
¼ C. Bisquick baking mix
1 C. brown sugar
½ tsp. salt
1 tsp. vinegar

¼ tsp. nutmeg
1½ C. Bisquick baking mix
½ C. milk
1/8 tsp. cinnamon

1 C. water
1 tsp. vanilla
1 T. butter or margarine

For Caramel Sauce: Blend baking mix, sugar and salt in saucepan. Stir in vinegar and water. Micro-cook until boils, stirring after every 2 minutes, cook until thickens. Remove from oven and add vanilla and butter. Cool.

For Filling: Place apples in ungreased square non-metalic pan. Sprinkle with ½ tsp cinnamon and the nutmeg. Stir baking mix and milk into a soft dough. Spread dough over apples. Sprinkle with 1/8 tsp. cinnamon. Pour Caramel Sauce over top. Micro-cook 12 minutes at full power.

APPLE NUT DESSERT

1 C. sugar
¾ C. flour
2 tsp. baking powder
¼ tsp. salt
½ C. evaporated milk
1 tsp. vanilla

½ C. nuts
3 C. chopped apples
2 T. brown sugar
⅓ C. flour
2 T. butter

In a 2-qt. bowl mix with fork the sugar, flour, salt and baking powder. Stir in the milk and vanilla; mix. Stir in the nuts and apples until coated with batter. Spread in a 9-inch square pan. Mix with fork, until crumbly the brown sugar, flour and butter. Sprinkle this over the apple batter. Bake in a 400° oven 30-35 minutes.

APPLE DESSERT

COMBINE:
¾ C. flour
1 C. brown sugar
1 ½ tsp. baking powder

½ tsp. salt
Dash of cinnamon

Stir in 2 unbeaten eggs, then fold in 1 ½ C. chopped tart apples and ¾ C. walnuts. Turn into greased 9-inch pie pan.

BAKED FRUIT

6 apples (or 2 C. applesauce)
2 C. peaches
2 C. pears
2 C. pineapple chunks
2 C. apricots

2 C. cherry pie filling
1/3 C. brown sugar
1 1/3 tsp. cinnamon
1/4 tsp. ground cloves

Mix all the fruit thoroughly with pie filling to coat evenly. Pour into 9 x 13-inch baking dish. Mix brown sugar, cinnamon and cloves and sprinkle over fruit. Bake at 350° for 30 to 45 minutes.

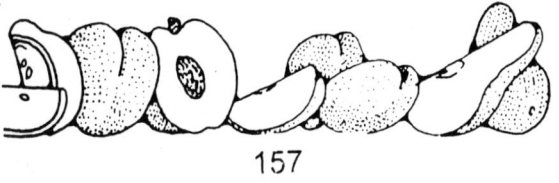

157

APPLE CAKE DESSERT

2 C. sugar
½ C. butter
2 eggs
2 C. flour
1 tsp. soda

2 tsp. cinnamon
1 tsp. nutmeg
1 tsp. salt
4 C. chopped apples

Cream sugar and butter. Add beaten eggs. Sift dry ingredients together and add egg to batter. Add apples and bake in greased and floured 9x13-inch pan for 1 hour. Bake at 350° for 15 minutes. Serve with whipped cream or ice cream.

SOUR CREAM APPLE SQUARES

2 C. flour
2 C. brown sugar
½ C. margarine (softened)
1 C. chopped nuts
1-2 tsp. cinnamon
1 tsp. soda

½ tsp. salt
1 C. sour cream
1 tsp. vanilla
1 egg
2 C. peeled, finely chopped apples

Heat oven to 350°. In large bowl, combine first 3 ingredients until crumbly. Stir in nuts, press 2¾ C. crumb mixture into ungreased 9x13-inch pan. To remaining mixture, add cinnamon, soda, salt, sour cream, vanilla and egg; blend well. Stir in apples. Spoon evenly over base. Bake 25-35 minutes, until toothpick inserted in center comes out clean. Cut into squares. Serve with whipped cream, if desired. Makes 12-15 squares.

Apple Cobbler

5 C. apples
1 C. sugar
1½ C. all-purpose flour
1 T. sugar
2 tsp. baking powder

½ tsp. salt
⅓ C. shortening
½ C. milk
½ tsp. cinnamon

Spread sliced apples in a 9x9-inch baking dish. Mix together 1 C. sugar and cinnamon; spread over sliced apples. Put in 400° oven for 10 minutes. Mix together flour, 1 T. sugar, baking powder, and salt. Cut in shortening. Beat egg, add milk to egg and add to dry ingredients. Drop over hot apples and sprinkle 1 T. sugar over batter. Bake at 400° for 25 minutes. NOTE: Other fruits may be used.

DUMPLINGS

APPLE DUMPLINGS

2 C. sugar	3 C. water
¼ tsp. cinnamon	¼ tsp. nutmeg
4 C. chopped apples	2 C. flour
4 tsp. baking powder	1 tsp. salt
1 stick oleo	⅔ C. milk

Boil sugar, water, cinnamon, and nutmeg 5 minutes. Mix oleo into flour, baking powder and salt until crumbly. Add chopped apples and milk. Stir in. Pour boiling mixture into 9x13-inch cake pan. Drop dough mixture into boiling mixture and bake in 350° oven until golden brown. (VARIATIONS: Substitute rhubarb for apples and leave out cinnamon and nutmeg. Substitute two No. 2½ cans peaches for apples. Use juice off peaches and 1 C. water and cut back sugar to 1 C.)

APPLE DUMPLINGS WITH CREAM

2 C. sugar
2 C. water
¼ tsp. cinnamon
¼ tsp. nutmeg
¼ C. butter
6 apples (or so, unpeeled)

2 C. flour
1 tsp. salt
2 tsp. baking powder
¾ C. shortening
½ C. milk

Make syrup of sugar, water, cinnamon and nutmeg. Add butter. Pare and core apples, slice. Sift flour, salt and baking powder; cut in shortening, add milk all at once and stir until moist. Roll ¼-inch thick; cut in 5-inch squares. Arrange apple slices on square; sprinkle generously with additional sugar, cinnamon and nutmeg. Dot with butter; fold corners to center, pinch edges together. Place in greased baking dish. Pour syrup over. Bake at 375° for 35 minutes. Serve hot with cream/milk. Makes 6-8 large dumplings.

SWEET APPLE DUMPLINGS

1½ C. sugar
1½ C. water
½ tsp. cinnamon
½ tsp. vanilla flavoring
3 T. butter
2 C. sifted flour

2 tsp. baking powder
1 tsp. salt
⅔ C. shortening
½ C. milk
6 whole apples (pared and cored)

Bring sugar, water and cinnamon to a boil. Add butter and vanilla; set aside. Sift flour, baking powder, and salt. Cut in shortening. Add milk, and stir until flour is moistened. Roll out on floured board to a 12x18-inch rectangle. Cut in 6-inch squares. Place an apple in each square and sprinkle with sugar and cinnamon. Dot with butter. Fold corners to center and pinch together. Place in 8x11-inch baking pan. Pour syrup over. Sprinkle with more sugar. Bake at 375° oven for 35 minutes or until apples are tender.

APPLE DUMPLINGS WITH SAUCE

2 ½ C. apples (peeled and chopped)   1 tsp. salt
2 C. flour   ¾ C. shortening
2 tsp. baking powder   ½ C. milk

SAUCE:
2 C. sugar
¼ C. butter   2 C. water

Make like pie dough and cut in six 5-inch squares. Put in apples, sugar and cinnamon, if wanted. Fold dough over apples.

For Sauce: Bring to boil 2 C. sugar, 2 C. water and ¼ C. butter and pour over dumplings. Bake 40 minutes at 375°.

YUMMY APPLE DUMPLINGS

SYRUP:
2 qts. water   2 C. sugar

Put water and sugar in Dutch oven or other large pan and let it come to a boil while making crust and filling.

CRUST:
2 C. flour   ⅓ C. shortening
1 tsp. salt   Water

Cream flour, salt and shortening. Add enough water to make pie crust. Roll into 12x16-inch rectangle and cut into 4-inch squares.

FILLING:
3 apples
Cinnamon

Sugar
Oleo

Quarter and peel apples. Slice 1 quarter onto each square of crust. Sprinkle each with 1 tsp. sugar and a dash of cinnamon. Put small dot of oleo on top of each and then seal the crust around each. Put into boiling syrup and simmer for 30 minutes.

MISC.

Apple Butter

2 C. unsweetened applesauce
1/2 C. sugar
1 tsp. cinnamon

1/4 tsp. allspice
1/8 tsp. ginger
1/8 tsp. cloves

Combine ingredients in a heavy 1 1/2-quart saucepan. Bring to a boil and cook for 30 minutes. Makes 1 1/4 cups.

CRAB APPLE PICKLES

1 gal. apples (washed and pricked)	2 sticks cinnamon
5 C. sugar	1 T. whole allspice
4 C. dark vinegar	½ T. whole cloves
3 C. water	Gauze bag

In large kettle mix sugar, vinegar, and water. Tie spices in gauze bag and add to syrup mixture. Bring syrup to a boil and cook until sugar dissolves. Remove from heat and cool. When cooled add apples (whole) and return to heat. Simmer until apples are tender, but not mushy. Remove from heat and let stand 12-18 hours. Remove apples from syrup and pack into hot jars. Heat syrup and pour over apples. Seal with hot lids.

NEED GIFTS?

Are you up a stump for some nice gifts for some nice people in your life? Here's a list of some of the best cookbooks in the western half of the Universe. Just check 'em off, stick a check in an envelope with this page, and we'll get your books off to you pronto. Oh, yes, add $2.00 for shipping and handling for the first book and then fifty cents more for each additional one. If you order over $30.00, forget the shipping and handling.

Mini Cookbooks
(Only 3-1/2 x 5) With Maxi Good Eatin' - 160 or 192 pages - $5.95

❏ Arizona Cooking
❏ Dakota Cooking
❏ Illinois Cooking
❏ Indiana Cooking
❏ Iowa Cookin'
❏ Kansas Cookin'
❏ Kentucky Cookin'
❏ Michigan Cooking
❏ Minnesota Cookin'
❏ Missouri Cookin'
❏ New Jersey Cooking
❏ New Mexico Cooking
❏ New York Cooking
❏ Ohio Cooking
❏ Pennsylvania Cooking
❏ Wisconsin Cooking
❏ Amish & Mennonite Strawberry Cookbook
❏ Aphrodisiac Cooking
❏ Apples! Apples! Apples!

❏ Apples Galore
❏ Berries! Berries! Berries!
❏ Berries Galore!
❏ Cherries! Cherries! Cherries!
❏ Citrus! Citrus! Citrus!
❏ Cooking with Cider
❏ Cooking with Fresh Herbs
❏ Cooking with Spirits
❏ Cooking with Garlic
❏ Cooking with Things Go Baa
❏ Cooking with Things Go Cluck
❏ Cooking with Things Go Moo
❏ Cooking with Things Go Oink
❏ Cooking with Things Go Splash
❏ Good Cookin' From the Plain People
❏ Hill Country Cookin'
❏ How to Make Salsa
❏ Kid Cookin'
❏ The Kid's Garden Fun Book

❏ Kid Pumpkin Fun Book
❏ Midwest Small Town Cookin'
❏ Muffins Cookbook
❏ Nuts! Nuts! Nuts!
❏ Off To College Cookbook
❏ Peaches! Peaches! Peaches!
❏ Pumpkins! Pumpkins! Pumpkins!
❏ Some Like It Hot
❏ Super Simple Cookin'
❏ Working Girl Cookbook
❏ Veggie Talk Coloring & Story Book $6.95

In-Between Cookbooks
(5 1/2 x 8 1/2) - 150 pages - $9.95

❏ The Adaptable Apple Cookbook
❏ Breads! Breads! Breads!
❏ Camp Cookin'
❏ Civil War Cookin', Stories, 'n Such
❏ Cooking Ala Nude
❏ Country Cooking Recipes from my Amish Heritage
❏ The Cow Puncher's Cookbook
❏ Eating Ohio
❏ Farmers Market Cookbook
❏ The Fire Fighters Cookbook
❏ Halloween Fun Book
❏ Herbal Cookery

- ☐ Hunting in the Nude Cookbook
- ☐ Ice Cream Cookbook
- ☐ Wil-kon-ge Inizan Maazina 'Igans
  (The Indian Moon Cookbook)
- ☐ Indian Cooking Cookbook
- ☐ Mad About Garlic
- ☐ Motorcycler's Wild Critter
  Cookbook
- ☐ Soccer Mom's Cookbook
- ☐ Shhhh Cookbook

- ☐ Turn of the Century Cooking
- ☐ Vegan Vegetarian Cookbook
- ☐ Depression Times Cookbook
- ☐ Dial-a-Dream Cookbook
- ☐ Flat out, Dirt Cheap Cookin'
- ☐ Hormone Helper Cookbook
- ☐ The I-got-Funner-things-to-

Biggie Cookbooks
(5-1/2 x 8-1/2) - 200 plus pages - $11.95
- ☐ A Cookbook for them what Ain't
  Done a Whole lot of Cookin'
- ☐ Aphrodisiac Cooking
- ☐ Back to the Supper Table Cookbook
- ☐ Cooking for One (ok, Maybe two)
- ☐ Covered Bridges Cookbook

Hearts 'N Tummies Cookbook Co.
1854 - 345th Ave
Wever, IA 52658
800-571-2665

Name_____

Address_____

_____

*You Iowa folks gotta kick in another 6% for Sales Tax.